DATA SCIENTIST AS A

STRATEGIST

Aligning Data Insights with Business Goals

Eretoru Nimi Robert

Published by:
Emphaloz Publishing House
www.emphaloz.com
publish@emphaloz.com

ISBN: 978-1-7430-6671-3

A catalogue record of this book will be available from the National Library of Nigeria.

Table Of Contents

Foreword

In the modern business landscape, the ability to harness data is not just an advantage, a necessity. Organizations today operate in an era where decisions made with the backing of data are more informed, reliable, and future-focused than ever before. The role of the data scientist has grown exponentially in this environment, evolving from a primarily technical function to one that sits at the intersection of analytics, strategy, and leadership. This shift is profound, and it signals the arrival of a new era where data scientists are no longer just number crunchers or analysts, but pivotal players in the strategic direction of a company. It is with this backdrop that Data Scientist as a Strategist: Aligning Data Insights with Business Goals emerges as a timely and essential guide for data professionals and business leaders alike. The central premise of this book is one that every executive, manager, and data scientist should embrace: the true power of data lies not just in its ability to generate insights, but in how those insights are applied to meet the goals and objectives of a business.

To bridge that gap, data scientists must adopt a mindset that goes beyond technical prowess, developing skills in communication, strategy, and cross-functional collaboration. The importance of this mindset cannot be overstated. Today's businesses, from tech giants to startups, are swimming in an ocean of data. But data without strategy is like a ship without a captain—it can drift aimlessly, yielding little value. Only when data is aligned with clear business goals does it become a strategic asset. This alignment, however, is no easy task. It requires data scientists to understand not just the technical aspects of data, but also the operational and financial metrics that define business success. It calls for them to speak the language of executives and understand the broader strategic vision of the company. In my own experience working with data teams and business leaders, I have witnessed firsthand how transformative it can be when data insights are properly aligned with business objectives. I've seen data scientists shift from being viewed as back-office support to becoming integral members of the executive team, contributing to strategic conversations and driving company-wide initiatives.

These data professionals are more than analysts, they are strategists. And in today's competitive marketplace, their influence can mean the difference between stagnation and growth. Data Scientist as a Strategist lays out a clear roadmap for making this transformation. It offers actionable advice on how data scientists can broaden their impact by mastering the art of strategic thinking. From learning the key performance indicators (KPIs) that business leaders care about, to understanding how to effectively communicate complex data insights to non-technical stakeholders, this book addresses the critical skills that are often missing from traditional data science training. The beauty of this book is that it doesn't just stop at the theoretical. It dives deep into real-world case studies and provides practical examples that illustrate how data has been used to drive business strategy in successful organizations. The case of Netflix, for example, demonstrates how data can be used not just to inform content recommendations but to guide larger business decisions about customer retention, content investment, and even market expansion.

Similarly, companies like Spotify and Amazon have shown how data science teams, when properly aligned with business strategy, can provide a competitive edge that allows them to dominate their industries. What makes this book especially valuable is its focus on the cross-functional nature of modern data work. No longer can data scientists operate in silos, detached from the broader organization. The most impactful data teams work in close collaboration with marketing, finance, product development, and operations, ensuring that data insights are relevant and actionable across departments. This cross-functional collaboration is a theme that resonates throughout the book, and it's one that any data professional or business leader would do well to internalize. One of the great challenges addressed in Data Scientist as a Strategist is the difficulty many organizations face in becoming truly data driven. While nearly every company today claims to value data, the reality is that many struggle to turn data insights into meaningful business outcomes.

This book tackles that challenge head-on by offering a detailed framework for overcoming common barriers such as organizational silos, lack of data literacy, and resistance to change. It provides a clear, actionable path for building a data-driven culture—one where insights are consistently aligned with business goals, and where every department, from the C-suite to the front lines, understands the strategic value of data. As you embark on this journey through the pages of this book, I encourage you to think not just about the technical skills required for success in data science, but also the strategic mindset that will set you apart in your career. Whether you are a seasoned data professional, a manager seeking to leverage data more effectively, or a business leader aiming to better understand the role of data in your company's strategy, this book will provide you with the tools and insights needed to thrive in the evolving world of data-driven decision-making. The future of business is data-driven, but only if we can effectively align data with business strategy. This book shows us how to do just that. By bridging the gap between data science and strategy, you can unlock the full potential of your organization's data, driving innovation, growth, and long-term success.

I am excited to see how this book will inspire and empower the next generation of data scientists and business leaders to work together in driving strategic, data-driven success.

Introduction

We live in an era where data has become the new currency of business. Every action, transaction, and interaction leaves behind a digital footprint that, when harnessed correctly, has the power to transform organizations and industries. In this fast-evolving landscape, businesses are no longer asking whether they should use data; they're asking how to use it strategically. That shift marks the beginning of a new chapter for data scientists. No longer confined to the role of technical analysts or data wranglers, today's data scientists are increasingly being called upon to be strategists—professionals who not only generate insights but also help shape the future direction of the business. This book, Data Scientist as a Strategist: Aligning Data Insights with Business Goals, is about that very transformation. It's about redefining the role of data scientists so they can evolve into key strategic partners who contribute meaningfully to their organization's long-term success. The data scientist who can connect their insights to the overarching goals of the business is no longer just part of a support function—they become a critical player in shaping business decisions, identifying new opportunities, and driving innovation.

The Evolving Role of the Data Scientist

Traditionally, data science has been seen as a highly technical discipline focused on creating models, running analyses, and generating reports. And while these skills remain crucial, they are no longer enough. The ability to code in Python, build machine learning models, or create stunning visualizations in Tableau is valuable, but it's only the foundation. What businesses need today is a more strategic application of these skills—a data scientist who not only understands the data but can also align their insights with business goals and objectives. In other words, data scientists must evolve into business strategists who can use data to shape decisions, drive business outcomes, and ultimately contribute to the success of the organization. This shift requires a change in mindset. Instead of viewing data science as a purely analytical function, data professionals need to see themselves as part of the broader business strategy. They need to ask questions like: How can our data drive revenue growth? How can we use our insights to reduce costs? How can data help us make smarter decisions, improve customer satisfaction, or gain a competitive advantage? These are the questions that leaders and executives are asking—and they need data scientists to provide the answers.

Why Business Alignment Matters

At its core, aligning data insights with business goals is about ensuring that the work of data scientists contributes directly to the success of the organization. Without this alignment, even the most sophisticated models and analyses can become irrelevant. Imagine a data team spending weeks or months developing a predictive model, only to find that it doesn't address the company's most pressing challenges or doesn't resonate with decision-makers. This misalignment is a common problem in many organizations. It's not that data scientists aren't skilled or that they aren't producing valuable insights—it's that those insights aren't being used in a way that impacts the bottom line. That's why aligning data with business strategy is critical. When data initiatives are aligned with business goals, they have a clear purpose, and their value is immediately understood by all stakeholders. This alignment ensures that data insights aren't just interesting, they're actionable, relevant, and essential to achieving the company's objectives. In practice, this means that data scientists need to be deeply familiar with the company's strategic goals. They need to understand how the business defines success, whether it's increasing revenue, reducing operational costs, expanding into new markets, or enhancing customer loyalty. And they need to think creatively about how data can support these goals.

The Gap Between Data and Decision-Making

Despite the growing importance of data, many organizations still struggle to become truly data driven. They might collect vast amounts of data, invest in analytics tools, and hire skilled data professionals, but there's often a disconnect between the data insights being generated and the decisions being made by business leaders. In many cases, this gap exists because data scientists and business leaders operate in silos—each with their own language, priorities, and expectations. For data scientists, the challenge is not just technical; it's about communication and collaboration. To be effective, data professionals need to be able to explain their insights in a way that resonates with non-technical stakeholders. This involves translating complex models and statistical outputs into actionable business recommendations that executives can act on. It's about telling a story with the data—one that is aligned with the company's strategic goals and provides clear, actionable insights. At the same time, business leaders need to become more data-literate. They need to understand not just the potential of data but also its limitations. They must ask the right questions and be willing to engage with data scientists to fully leverage the value of their insights. This mutual understanding is key to bridging the gap between data science and decision-making.

This book is a comprehensive guide for data scientists, business leaders, and managers who want to close the gap between data insights and business strategy. It provides actionable steps for building a stronger connection between data and business goals, covering everything from the basics of business literacy for data professionals to advanced strategies for aligning data science projects with the company's overall direction.

Throughout the book, we will explore key concepts such as:

Understanding business objectives: How to align data projects with strategic priorities.

Effective communication: How to present data in a way that influences decision-makers and drives action.

Building a data-driven culture: How to create an environment where data informs every decision.

Cross-functional collaboration: How data teams can work effectively with other departments to ensure alignment and impact.

Advanced analytics in strategy: How AI and machine learning can support long-term business planning.

In each chapter, we'll provide real-world examples and case studies from companies that have successfully aligned their data initiatives with their business strategy. You'll learn how leading companies use data to drive decision-making at the highest levels and how you can apply those lessons to your own organization. As you progress through this book, you will gain the tools and insights needed to not only excel in the technical aspects of data science but also to contribute meaningfully to your organization's strategic direction. Whether you're a seasoned data professional or a business leader looking to understand how data can drive growth, this book will help you navigate the intersection of data and strategy. In the end, the goal is clear: to equip you with the knowledge and skills to be a data scientist who isn't just focused on analytics but who is also a strategic partner in achieving business success. Welcome to the future of data science—a future where data and strategy are in perfect alignment.

CHAPTER 1

The Evolving Role of Data Science in Business

Data science has fundamentally changed the way businesses operate, offering tools and insights that allow companies to make more informed decisions, predict future trends, and enhance efficiency. But the role of the data scientist is no longer confined to number-crunching and producing insights from raw data. Data scientists are now seen as integral members of leadership teams, playing a crucial role in guiding the strategic direction of their organizations. In this chapter, we will explore how the role of the data scientist has evolved from being a purely technical function to becoming a vital player in business strategy.

From Data Analysis to Strategic Partner

For many years, data scientists were viewed primarily as technical experts responsible for extracting insights from complex datasets. This role was valuable but often limited to providing reports or performing analyses that others in the organization could use to make decisions. Data scientists, in the early years of the discipline,

1

were typically part of IT or research teams, focused more on operational issues and less on strategic alignment with the company's broader goals. However, the growing importance of data in business decision-making has expanded the role of data scientists. The shift began as businesses started recognizing the competitive advantage of leveraging data not just for analysis, but as a core asset in strategy formation. Executives began looking to data scientists not only to provide insights but to help shape those insights into actionable strategies. Data professionals were no longer seen as a back-office function but as partners in shaping business outcomes. Today, a data scientist who limits their role to analysis alone risks being left behind. The demands of modern business require a new set of skills beyond technical expertise. Data scientists are now expected to collaborate with different business functions, communicate effectively with leadership, and most importantly, align their work with the organization's broader strategic goals. This shift means that data scientists must understand the business they are working in, speak the language of executives, and connect data work to the larger objectives of the company.

The Strategic Imperative of Data

The rise of big data and the increasing sophistication of analytics tools have turned data into a central part of most business strategies. In this environment, data scientists must develop a more strategic mindset. They are no longer expected simply to answer technical questions like *"What happened?"* or *"What is likely to*

2

happen?" Instead, they need to address the more profound question of *"How can we use this data to shape the future of the business?"* A key part of this evolution is understanding the business context in which data insights are applied. Without this understanding, data science can become disconnected from the actual needs of the business, rendering even the most complex models or analyses ineffective. Strategic thinking means being able to interpret the business environment, identify where data can add value, and anticipate the kind of decisions executives need to make. This is a significant departure from traditional data science roles, which focused predominantly on creating models and extracting insights without necessarily engaging in the application of those insights in real-world decision-making. For example, a data scientist working for an e-commerce company might have historically been tasked with identifying customer trends or forecasting sales. Today, that same data scientist is expected to not only identify trends but also provide strategic recommendations on how to capitalize on those trends to improve customer retention, optimize marketing spending, or expand into new markets. The insights themselves are not enough, the value comes from connecting those insights to tangible business outcomes.

The Skillset Shift: Beyond Technical Expertise

One of the most significant changes in the role of the data scientist is the skillset required to succeed. Traditionally, data scientists were expected to have expertise in statistics, machine learning, and programming languages such as Python or R. While these skills remain foundational, they are no longer sufficient to thrive in today's business environment. To truly contribute to strategy, data scientists must also develop a range of non-technical skills that allow them to communicate effectively with executives, collaborate with other departments, and think in terms of business outcomes. These skills include:

Business Acumen: Understanding the core drivers of the business is essential for aligning data projects with strategic goals. Data scientists need to learn how to read financial statements, grasp key performance indicators (KPIs), and understand market trends. This allows them to connect their technical work to the bigger picture, ensuring that their insights are relevant to the company's objectives.

Communication Skills: One of the biggest challenges data scientists' faces is communicating complex insights to non-technical stakeholders. Data scientists must be able to distill their findings into clear, actionable recommendations that resonate with executives and align with the company's strategic goals. This requires not just storytelling, but the ability to frame data in the context of business priorities.

Collaboration: Modern businesses operate in a highly collaborative environment, and data scientists must work closely with a variety of departments, including marketing, operations, and product development. Being able to collaborate effectively with these teams ensures that data insights are embedded into business processes and that the data function is not siloed from the rest of the organization.

Strategic Thinking: To make the leap from technical expert to strategic partner, data scientists must cultivate the ability to think long-term and align their work with broader business objectives. This means anticipating the needs of the business, understanding competitive pressures, and identifying where data can provide a strategic advantage.

The Data Scientist as a Business Leader

As the role of the data scientist evolves, so does the expectation that data professionals will take on leadership roles within their organizations. This is particularly true in companies where data has become a critical asset, such as tech firms, financial institutions, and e-commerce businesses. In these environments, data scientists are not just providing support, they are helping shape the overall direction of the company. This shift is reflected in the growing trend of data scientists taking on leadership roles, such as Chief Data Officers (CDOs) or Chief Analytics Officers (CAOs). These roles highlight the strategic importance of data science within the company, placing data at the center of decision-making processes. CDOs and CAOs are responsible not just for managing the technical aspects of data but for ensuring that data is used to drive strategic initiatives across the organization. One of the key challenges for data scientists in leadership roles is balancing technical expertise with business strategy. While it's important to maintain a deep understanding of the technical aspects of data science, leaders in these roles must also be able to engage with the business side of the organization, influencing strategy, guiding decision-making, and ensuring that data initiatives are aligned with broader business goals.

Data-Driven Strategy in Action

A powerful example of how the role of the data scientist has evolved can be seen in the way companies like Amazon and Netflix use data to shape their business strategies. At Amazon, data is not just used to optimize operational processes, it's at the heart of every major business decision. Data scientists at Amazon work closely with leadership to identify new growth opportunities, improve customer experience, and drive innovation. Their insights have led to the development of major products like Amazon Prime, which was driven by data analysis showing that customers who received faster shipping were more likely to make repeat purchases. Similarly, at Netflix, data scientists are deeply involved in content strategy, helping to determine which shows to invest in based on detailed analyses of viewer behavior. Netflix's recommendation engine, which uses predictive analytics to suggest shows and movies to users, is a well-known example of how data scientists at the company are driving customer engagement. But beyond recommendations, Netflix data scientists work closely with executives to identify larger strategic opportunities, such as market expansion or customer retention initiatives. In both of these companies, data scientists are not just contributors to specific projects, they are central to the company's strategic direction. Their ability to align data insights with business goals has made them invaluable partners in driving growth and innovation.

The New Role of Data Scientists

As data becomes an integral part of business strategy, the role of the data scientist must continue to evolve. No longer can data professionals remain purely focused on technical work—they must develop the skills needed to contribute to the broader strategic goals of their organizations. This requires a shift in mindset, from technical expert to business strategist. In the chapters that follow, we will explore the specific skills and strategies that data scientists need to master in order to align their work with business goals. From understanding key business metrics to developing effective communication strategies, this book will provide a comprehensive guide for data scientists who want to take their careers to the next level and become strategic leaders in their organizations. The journey from data analysis to strategic leadership is one that requires not just technical expertise, but also business acumen, communication skills, and a deep understanding of how data can drive business success. By mastering these skills, data scientists can transform themselves into essential partners in shaping the future of their organizations.

CHAPTER 2

Business Fundamentals for Data Scientists

As data science evolves, the demands placed on data scientists have also shifted. Gone are the days when data scientists could focus exclusively on their technical skills—coding, statistical analysis, and machine learning models. Today, they must also understand the business side of their organization in order to provide insights that drive real-world decisions. This chapter is designed to equip data scientists with a deeper understanding of the business fundamentals needed to align their work with broader organizational goals. While technical expertise remains essential, it is equally important for data scientists to grasp how businesses operate, generate value, and measure success. By gaining a solid understanding of business models, key performance indicators (KPIs), and financial metrics, data scientists can ensure their work directly contributes to the strategic priorities of the business.

Understanding Business Models and Value Creation

At the heart of every business lies a business model, the blueprint for how the company generates value, serves its customers, and sustains profitability. Business models differ widely across industries, and data scientists need to have a basic understanding of these models to tailor their analyses to the company's goals.

Business-to-Business (B2B) vs. Business-to-Consumer (B2C) Models

B2B companies typically sell products or services to other businesses, which often involves longer sales cycles, complex contracts, and highly specialized offerings. In this context, data scientists may focus on optimizing lead generation, customer segmentation, or pricing strategies based on data from large enterprise clients. Metrics like customer acquisition cost (CAC) and lifetime value (LTV) can be critical in B2B settings. In contrast, B2C companies sell directly to individual consumers, often at a larger scale but with lower transaction values. Here, data scientists may focus on understanding customer behavior, improving marketing strategies, and personalizing product recommendations. In B2C companies, metrics like conversion rates, customer churn, and engagement rates are often central to decision-making. Understanding the nuances of your company's business model is key to identifying the right data-driven opportunities. For example, if you are working at a B2B company, your insights might need to focus on optimizing the sales pipeline or identifying high-value customer segments. In a B2C environment, you might be more focused on real-time customer behavior or designing predictive models for personalization.

Value Creation in Business: Every business seeks to create value, either for customers, stakeholders, or shareholders. As a data scientist, your job is to help the business identify ways to create, capture, and sustain that value through data-driven insights. In many cases, this means identifying opportunities for increased efficiency, revenue generation, or customer satisfaction. For instance, in an e-commerce company, data scientists might focus on optimizing the supply chain to reduce costs or using data to enhance the customer shopping experience, thereby increasing sales and customer loyalty. In a manufacturing business, data scientists might look at production data to minimize waste and improve productivity. In each case, the key is to understand how the business defines value and how data can help enhance that value.

The Role of KPIs (Key Performance Indicators)

Key performance indicators (KPIs) are the metrics that businesses use to track their progress toward strategic goals. For data scientists, understanding KPIs is crucial because they provide a clear link between data insights and business outcomes. Without aligning data projects to the KPIs that matter to the business, even the most sophisticated analysis can fail to drive meaningful action. Why KPIs

Matter: KPIs are often seen as the "language" of business leaders—they offer a concise way to measure success, identify areas of improvement, and make data-driven decisions. By focusing on the KPIs that are most relevant to the company's strategic goals, data scientists can ensure that their analyses and models are closely tied to the business' success. For example, a retail company may track KPIs like same-store sales growth, inventory turnover, or average transaction value to assess the health of its business. A software-as-a-service (SaaS) company may prioritize metrics like monthly recurring revenue (MRR), customer churn, or customer satisfaction scores. In both cases, data scientists need to focus on these key metrics when conducting their analyses, as they offer a direct link between data insights and the company's strategic goals.

Aligning Data Projects with KPIs: The best way for data scientists to ensure their work is aligned with business objectives is to directly tie their projects to the company's KPIs. If the KPI is to reduce customer churn, for example, the data team might develop predictive models to identify customers at risk of leaving and suggest interventions. If the KPI is to increase revenue, data scientists might focus on identifying high-value customer segments or recommending strategies to optimize pricing. Aligning data projects with KPIs ensures that the insights generated are actionable and relevant to the business' priorities. It also helps bridge the gap between technical analysis and business decision-making, ensuring that data plays a strategic role in driving the company forward.

Financial Metrics Data Scientists Must Know

To truly align data science with business strategy, it's essential for data scientists to understand key financial metrics. These metrics are often at the core of how businesses assess performance and make strategic decisions. By grasping these concepts, data scientists can develop a deeper understanding of what drives business success and how data insights can be used to support it.

Revenue and Profit Margins: Revenue is the total income generated from the sale of goods or services. Data scientists may be involved in projects that aim to grow revenue, such as analyzing sales trends, optimizing pricing strategies, or identifying new market opportunities. Profit margins are a measure of how much of the revenue is kept as profit after accounting for expenses. Gross profit margin, operating profit margin, and net profit margin are commonly used metrics. Data science can play a critical role in improving profit margins, for example, by identifying cost-saving opportunities in supply chains or by optimizing operations.

Return on Investment (ROI): ROI measures the profitability of an investment relative to its cost. This is a crucial metric for executives who need to assess the potential return from various initiatives, whether they are marketing campaigns, product launches, or technology investments. Data scientists can contribute to ROI calculations by providing predictive models and insights that forecast the likely impact of certain initiatives and optimize resource allocation. For instance, if a company is considering investing in a new customer acquisition strategy, a data scientist can analyze historical data to estimate how effective this new strategy might be, what customer segments to target, and what kind of ROI the company can expect.

Customer Lifetime Value (CLTV): CLTV measures the total value a customer is expected to bring to the company over their entire relationship. This metric is particularly important in subscription-based businesses or industries with recurring customers. Understanding CLTV allows businesses to make informed decisions about customer acquisition, retention, and marketing expenses. Data scientists are instrumental in calculating and predicting CLTV, using models that factor in customer behavior, purchase frequency, and churn risk.

Cash Flow and Cost Control: Cash flow represents the movement of money in and out of a business. Positive cash flow ensures that a business has the resources to sustain operations and invest in growth. Data scientists can help optimize cash flow by analyzing operational efficiencies, forecasting future cash flows, and identifying cost-saving measures. In some cases, predictive models can be used to anticipate periods of negative cash flow, allowing businesses to take preventive measures. Understanding financial metrics like these allows data scientists to offer more strategic recommendations that align with the business's overall goals. It

14

helps ensure that data-driven initiatives don't just sound impressive but also translate into measurable business outcomes.

Mapping Data Science Projects for Business Objectives

One of the most significant challenges data scientists' faces is ensuring that their work is aligned with the strategic goals of the business. Too often, data science teams focus on interesting or technically challenging projects that, while valuable from a research perspective, fail to have a tangible impact on the business. To avoid this, data scientists need to adopt a more structured approach to aligning their projects with the company's business objectives.

Start with the Business Problem: The first step in aligning data projects with business objectives is to clearly define the business problem that needs to be solved. This requires close collaboration with stakeholders from various departments, including marketing, finance, operations, and leadership. Understanding the pain points and challenges faced by different parts of the organization helps data scientists identify where their skills can have the greatest impact. For example, if a company is struggling with customer churn, the business problem might be defined as: "How can we predict which customers are likely to churn, and what can we do to prevent it?" Once the problem is clearly defined, the data team can begin developing predictive models or identifying patterns in customer behavior that might inform retention strategies.

Identify Relevant Data Sources: Once the business problem is defined, the next step is to identify the data sources that are relevant to solving the problem. This might involve internal data, such as transaction histories or customer feedback, as well as external data, such as market trends or demographic information. Data scientists must ensure that the data they are using is reliable, up-to-date, and relevant to the specific business challenge at hand. In the case of customer churn, relevant data might include purchase history, engagement metrics, customer service interactions, and demographic data. By analyzing this data, the data team can begin to identify patterns that signal when a customer is at risk of churning.

Development and Test Hypotheses: Data science projects should be approached with a clear hypothesis in mind. In the case of customer churn, the hypothesis might be: "Customers who have reduced their purchase frequency by 50% in the past six months are more likely to churn." By testing this hypothesis using data, the team can either confirm or reject it, providing valuable insights into the factors driving customer churn. Hypothesis-driven analysis helps ensure that data projects are focused on answering specific business questions, rather than conducting open-ended exploration. This approach also provides a clear framework for measuring the success of the project, as the results can be directly compared to the original hypothesis.

Communicating Insights to Stakeholders: The final step in aligning data science projects with business objectives is to communicate the results effectively to stakeholders. Data scientists must be able to explain their findings in a way that resonates with business leaders, focusing not just on the technical aspects of the analysis but on the practical implications for the business. For example, if the data analysis reveals that customers with certain behavioral patterns are more likely to churn, the data team must present this insight in a way that helps the marketing or customer service team take action. This might involve recommending targeted retention campaigns for at-risk customers or suggesting changes to the customer service process to improve satisfaction.

Bridging the Gap Between Data Science and Business

For data scientists to have a real impact on their organizations, they must move beyond their technical expertise and develop a solid understanding of business fundamentals. By learning to navigate business models, KPIs, and financial metrics, data scientists can ensure that their work is aligned with the strategic goals of the company. Moreover, by focusing on solving specific business problems and communicating their insights effectively to stakeholders, data scientists can become essential partners in driving business success. In the chapters to come, we will explore more advanced strategies for aligning data science with business objectives, from effective communication and collaboration to building a data-driven culture. But it all starts with understanding the

17

fundamentals of how businesses operate and how data can be used to drive value. By mastering these concepts, data scientists can take the first step toward becoming strategic leaders in their organizations.

CHAPTER 3

Bridging the Communication Gap: Data Literacy for Executives

In an era where data is the driving force behind decision-making, the ability to communicate data insights effectively is as critical as the insights themselves. For data scientists, having a deep understanding of analytics, machine learning, and algorithms is essential. However, the real impact of data science is often determined by how well those insights are conveyed to non-technical stakeholders, especially business executives. These stakeholders—CEOs, CFOs, CMOs, and other decision-makers—are the ones who turn data-driven insights into strategic actions. Yet, one of the greatest challenges data professionals' faces is bridging the communication gap between technical complexity and business decision-making. This chapter explores the importance of data literacy for executives, the art of simplifying complex data for non-technical stakeholders, and effective strategies for storytelling and data visualization. By enhancing their communication skills, data scientists can ensure that their insights lead to meaningful actions, driving real business results.

The Importance of Data Literacy for Executives

In many organizations, there is a significant gap between the technical expertise of data scientists and the business acumen of executives. While executives are responsible for making high-level strategic decisions, they often lack the technical background to fully understand the nuances of data analysis. Conversely, data scientists may struggle to translate their findings into actionable insights that resonate with business leaders. This disconnect can lead to missed opportunities, misaligned goals, and ineffective decision-making. Why Data Literacy Matters: Data literacy refers to the ability to read, understand, and use data effectively in decision-making. For executives, being data literate does not mean having the technical skills to run algorithms or write code, but rather the ability to interpret data insights, ask the right questions, and make informed decisions based on the data presented.

In a data-driven organization, executives who possess a basic level of data literacy are better equipped to leverage the full potential of data science. They can engage in more meaningful conversations with their data teams, understand the limitations and possibilities of data, and make strategic decisions that are grounded in evidence. Consider the role of a Chief Marketing Officer (CMO) in a large retail company. The CMO may not need to know the intricacies of machine learning algorithms, but they do need to understand the key metrics that data scientists provide, such as customer lifetime value (CLTV), acquisition costs, and conversion rates. With a foundation in data literacy, the CMO can collaborate more effectively with the data team to design targeted marketing campaigns, optimize spending, and improve customer engagement.

The Data-Driven Executive: Executives who are data-literate have a clear advantage over those who are not. In fast-paced industries where decisions need to be made quickly and often in the face of uncertainty, data-literate executives can cut through the noise and focus on the most relevant data to inform their strategies. They can also challenge data scientists to go beyond surface-level insights and dig deeper into the root causes of business problems. For example, a CFO who understands data might question why a specific metric is trending downward and ask the data team to explore potential underlying factors, such as shifts in customer behavior, operational inefficiencies, or market changes. Without this level of engagement, the data scientist might present only surface-level insights, missing the opportunity to identify deeper issues.

Cultivating Data Literacy in the C-Suite: Data scientists can play a key role in cultivating data literacy among executives. This involves not only providing insights but also educating decision-makers on how to interpret and apply those insights in a business context. While formal data literacy training programs can be helpful, the most effective approach is often hands-on learning. Data scientists should take every opportunity to explain the reasoning behind their analyses, describe the limitations of certain models, and encourage executives to ask questions about the data. Over time, this fosters a more collaborative relationship between data teams and business leaders, enhancing the organization's overall ability to make data-driven decisions.

Simplifying Complex Data for Non-Technical Stakeholders

One of the greatest challenges data scientists' faces is translating complex analyses into language that non-technical stakeholders can understand. While data professionals are often comfortable with statistical terms, machine learning algorithms, and technical jargon, these concepts can be overwhelming for business leaders who are focused on strategy, operations, and growth. To drive meaningful action, data scientists must learn to simplify their findings without losing the integrity of the data.

The Challenge of Complexity: Data science, by its nature, deals with complex problems and sophisticated methodologies. Predictive models, neural networks, regression analyses, and clustering algorithms are essential tools in the data scientist's toolkit, but they can be difficult to explain to someone without a technical background. As a result, data scientists often struggle to communicate the full value of their work in a way that resonates with executives. For example, a data scientist might develop a machine learning model to predict customer churn with high accuracy, but presenting the technical details of the model to a CEO is unlikely to be effective. Instead, the data scientist needs to focus on the key takeaway: the model predicts which customers are most at risk of leaving, and the business can use this information to target retention efforts. By simplifying the message, the data scientist can ensure that the insight is understood and acted upon.

Focusing on Business Impact: The key to simplifying complex data is to focus on the business impact rather than the technical process. Executives care about outcomes—how the insights will help the company increase revenue, reduce costs, improve customer satisfaction, or gain a competitive edge. While it's important to maintain transparency about the methods used, data scientists should prioritize the "so what" factor: What does this data mean for the business? What actions should the company take as a result? Consider a scenario where a data scientist has identified a correlation between customer demographics and product preferences. Rather than explaining the statistical model used to identify this correlation, the data scientist should focus on the actionable insight: "Our analysis shows that customers aged 25-35 are more likely to purchase our premium product. We recommend targeting this demographic in our next marketing campaign to increase sales."

Using Analogies and Metaphors: One effective way to simplify complex data is to use analogies and metaphors that relate to the business. By comparing data insights to familiar concepts, data scientists can make abstract ideas more concrete and relatable for non-technical stakeholders. For instance, when explaining the concept of machine learning, a data scientist might compare it to teaching a child how to ride a bike. Just as a child learns from trial and error, adjusting their balance and speed until they master the skill, a machine learning model learns from patterns in data, improving its predictions over time. By using familiar analogies, data scientists can make complex concepts more accessible to executives, helping them understand the value of the insights being presented.

The Art of Data Storytelling

Data storytelling is a powerful tool that enables data scientists to turn raw data into compelling narratives that drive decision-making. By combining data insights with a clear, engaging narrative, data scientists can capture the attention of executives and ensure that their findings lead to action. Data storytelling goes beyond simply presenting numbers and charts—it involves crafting a story that highlights the business problem, presents the data as evidence, and provides a clear path forward.

Why Storytelling Matters: Humans are naturally drawn to stories. While numbers and statistics provide valuable information, they don't always resonate on an emotional or intuitive level. Stories, on the other hand, can make data more relatable, helping decision-makers understand the significance of the insights and motivating them to take action. For example, instead of saying, *"Our analysis shows a 15% increase in customer churn over the past quarter,"* a data scientist might frame the insight as a story: *"Over the past three months, we've seen an increasing number of our most loyal customers cancel their subscriptions. These customers represent a significant portion of our revenue, and if this trend continues, we could see a major impact on our bottom line. However, we've identified key patterns in their behavior that suggest targeted interventions could reverse this trend."* In this example, the data is presented within the context of a narrative that highlights the problem, its implications, and the potential solution. This approach makes the data more engaging and actionable for executives.

Crafting a Data-Driven Narrative: A successful data story follows a clear structure, much like any other narrative. It typically includes the following elements:

The Problem: Every good story starts with a problem that needs to be solved. In the context of data storytelling, this could be a business challenge such as declining sales, high customer churn, or inefficiencies in the supply chain. By framing the data within the context of a problem, data scientists can capture the attention of executives and create a sense of urgency.

The Data as Evidence: Once the problem is established, the next step is to present the data as evidence. This is where the data scientist shares their analysis, highlighting the key insights that shed light on the problem. It's important to focus on the most relevant data points, rather than overwhelming stakeholders with too much information.

The Solution: After presenting the data, the narrative should transition to the solution. What actions should the business take based on the data? This could include recommendations for strategic changes, process improvements, or new initiatives. The solution should be clear, actionable, and directly tied to the data insights.

The Impact: Finally, the data story should conclude with a discussion of the potential impact. How will the recommended actions affect the business? This could involve projected revenue increases, cost savings, or improvements in customer satisfaction. By quantifying the potential impact, data scientists can help executives understand the value of acting on the insights.

Engaging with Visualization: Effective data storytelling often involves the use of visual aids to make the narrative more compelling. Data visualization tools, such as charts, graphs, and infographics, help executives grasp complex data more quickly and clearly. However, data scientists must be careful not to overwhelm their audience with overly detailed or complicated visuals. Instead, they should focus on creating clear, simple visualizations that highlight the most important insights. For example, instead of presenting a complex scatter plot with multiple variables, a data scientist might use a simple bar chart to show how different customer segments contribute to revenue. By focusing on clarity and simplicity, data scientists can ensure that their visualizations enhance the narrative rather than detract from it.

Effective Communication Strategies for Data Scientists

Effective communication is not just about simplifying data or telling a good story, it's about creating a dialogue between data scientists and executives. By fostering open communication, data scientists can ensure that their insights are understood, valued, and acted upon. Here are some strategies for improving communication between data teams and business leaders:

Tailoring the Message to the Audience: Not all executives have the same level of data literacy or interest in technical details. Data scientists need to tailor their messages to the specific audience they are addressing. For example, a CEO might be more interested in high-level insights and strategic recommendations, while a CFO might want to dive deeper into financial metrics and ROI calculations. Understanding the audience's priorities and concerns allows data scientists to deliver more relevant and impactful messages.

Encouraging Two-Way Communication: Communication should not be a one-way street. Data scientists should encourage executives to ask questions, challenge assumptions, and provide feedback. This creates a more collaborative environment where data-driven decisions are made in partnership with business leaders. It also helps data scientists refine their analyses by incorporating the business perspective.

Building Trust Through Transparency: Data scientists should be transparent about the limitations of their analyses and the assumptions behind their models. By acknowledging uncertainty and potential biases in the data, they can build trust with executives and ensure that decisions are based on a clear understanding of the data's strengths and weaknesses. Transparency also encourages more informed discussions about risk and opportunity.

The Key to Data-Driven Decision-Making

Bridging the communication gap between data scientists and executives is critical to the success of any data-driven organization. While data scientists must have the technical skills to generate insights, they must also develop the ability to communicate those insights in a way that resonates with non-technical stakeholders. By focusing on business impact, simplifying complex data, and using storytelling and visualization to engage executives, data scientists can ensure that their work drives real business outcomes. As we continue through the book, we will explore how data scientists can further enhance their influence within organizations by fostering collaboration across teams, aligning data projects with business goals, and overcoming common challenges in building a data-driven culture. But the foundation of all these efforts is effective communication, the key to turning data insights into strategic action.

CHAPTER 4

Building a Data-Driven Culture

The shift toward data-driven decision-making has become a defining feature of modern organizations. In today's competitive landscape, businesses are increasingly relying on data not just to inform isolated decisions but to drive entire strategies. However, becoming a truly data-driven organization requires more than just hiring skilled data scientists or investing in the latest analytics tools—it requires building a culture where data is valued, understood, and used consistently across all levels of the business. This chapter focuses on how to build a data-driven culture, exploring the key elements needed to create an environment where data informs every decision and is embedded in the organization's DNA.

Why Culture Matters

Culture is often described as "the way we do things around here," and it plays a critical role in how organizations operate. In the context of data-driven decision-making, culture refers to how deeply the use of data is ingrained in everyday business practices. It's not enough for a company to claim that it values data; it must actively foster an environment where data is accessible, understood, and used by everyone—from entry-level employees to C-suite executives.

The Role of Culture in Decision-Making: Organizations with a strong data-driven culture don't rely on intuition or gut feelings to make decisions. Instead, they turn to data to guide their choices, whether it's launching a new product, entering a new market, or optimizing internal processes. In these organizations, data is seen as a strategic asset, and every decision is backed by evidence. However, building this kind of culture takes time and effort. Many companies face challenges when attempting to transition from a gut-driven to a data-driven mindset. These challenges can include resistance from employees, a lack of data literacy, siloed departments, and leadership that doesn't fully embrace the potential of data. Overcoming these hurdles requires a comprehensive approach that involves not just technology but also people and processes.

Data-Driven Culture vs. Data Availability: It's important to distinguish between simply having access to data and actually being data-driven. Many organizations have vast amounts of data but fail to use it effectively in decision-making. A true data-driven culture ensures that data is not only available but also used consistently to drive key business decisions. For instance, a company might have access to customer data, but if marketing decisions are still being made based on intuition or past experiences, the company isn't truly leveraging its data. A data-driven culture ensures that insights from data are integrated into the decision-making process at every level of the organization. This cultural shift can lead to better, more informed decisions that improve performance and drive growth.

Elements of a Data-Driven Culture

Building a data-driven culture requires focusing on several key elements that together create an environment where data is at the heart of the decision-making process. These elements include leadership commitment, data accessibility, employee engagement, cross-functional collaboration, and continuous learning.

1. Leadership Commitment: The foundation of any successful cultural transformation begins with leadership. For a company to become data-driven, its leaders must not only support the use of data but actively champion it. Executives and managers must lead by example, using data to inform their own decisions and encouraging their teams to do the same. Leadership commitment goes beyond providing verbal support for data initiatives—it involves setting clear expectations, allocating resources, and holding teams accountable for using data in their work. Leaders who embrace data-driven decision-making create a trickle-down effect, influencing the behavior of the entire organization. Consider a CEO who regularly reviews business performance metrics during executive meetings and expects each department head to present data-backed reports.

This sets the tone for the rest of the company, demonstrating that data isn't just a tool for analysts' integral to how the organization operates.

2. Data Accessibility: For a data-driven culture to flourish, employees need access to data. This means not only ensuring that data is available but also that it's easily accessible to everyone who needs it, regardless of their technical expertise. Data silos—where data is locked away within specific departments or systems—are one of the biggest obstacles to building a data-driven culture. When data is fragmented or difficult to access, it's nearly impossible for employees to use it effectively in their decision-making. To address this challenge, organizations need to implement systems that promote data sharing and transparency. This might involve adopting cloud-based data platforms that allow employees from different departments to access and analyze data in real time. It's also important to ensure that the data is clean, well-organized, and structured in a way that makes it easy to use. For example, an e-commerce company may collect vast amounts of customer data, but if that data is scattered across different systems (e.g. marketing tools, customer service platforms, and sales databases), it becomes difficult for teams to get a complete picture of the customer journey. By centralizing the data in a shared platform, the company can enable cross-functional teams to access the information they need to make informed decisions.

3. Employee Engagement and Data Literacy: A data-driven culture cannot thrive without the active participation of employees at all levels. However, many employees, particularly those without a technical background, may feel intimidated by data or unsure of how to use it in their roles. This is where data literacy comes into play. Data literacy refers to the ability to read, understand, and work with data. While not every employee needs to become a data scientist, everyone in a data-driven organization should have a basic level of data literacy. This includes understanding key metrics, knowing how to interpret data visualizations, and being able to ask the right questions of data analysts and scientists. To foster data literacy, companies should invest in training programs that equip employees with the skills they need to use data effectively. This might involve workshops, online courses, or hands-on training sessions that teach employees how to work with the data tools available to them. Additionally, companies can create resources such as data glossaries or cheat sheets to help employees navigate common data terms and concepts. By improving data literacy, organizations can empower employees to take ownership of data-driven decision-making in their roles. This not only enhances the quality of decisions being made but also increases employee engagement, as individuals feel more confident and capable when working with data.

4. Cross-Functional Collaboration: Data-driven decision-making often requires collaboration across multiple departments, as insights from data frequently span various functions within a company. For example, optimizing a marketing campaign may involve input from marketing, sales, customer service, and data analytics teams. In a data-driven culture, cross-functional collaboration is essential to ensure that data is shared and leveraged effectively across the organization. Breaking down silos between departments is critical for creating an environment where data flows freely and is used to inform decisions at every level. This can be achieved through regular cross-departmental meetings, data-sharing initiatives, and collaborative tools that allow teams to work together on data projects. For instance, a retail company looking to improve its customer experience might bring together data scientists, product managers, and customer service representatives to analyze customer feedback data. By combining the insights from each department, the company can develop a more comprehensive strategy for enhancing the customer journey.

5. Continuous Learning and Adaptation: Data science and analytics are constantly evolving fields, and staying up to date with the latest tools, methodologies, and trends is essential for maintaining a competitive edge. In a data-driven culture, organizations prioritize continuous learning and encourage employees to develop their data skills over time. This could involve offering opportunities for professional development, such as attending industry conferences, participating in data workshops, or pursuing advanced certifications in data analytics. Companies might also create internal data communities where employees can share best practices, collaborate on data projects, and learn from one another. Continuous learning isn't just about technical skills, it's also about fostering a mindset of curiosity and experimentation. In a data-driven culture, employees are encouraged to explore new ideas, test hypotheses, and learn from both successes and failures. This mindset is key to driving innovation and ensuring that the organization remains adaptable in a rapidly changing business environment.

Challenges in Building a Data-Driven Culture

While the benefits of building a data-driven culture are clear, the process is not without its challenges. Organizations often encounter resistance from employees, technical limitations, and cultural inertia that can slow down the transition to a more data-driven approach. Understanding and addressing these challenges is critical for success.

1. Resistance to Change: One of the most common obstacles to building a data-driven culture is resistance from employees who are accustomed to making decisions based on intuition or experience. In some cases, employees may feel threatened by data, believing that it could replace their expertise or undermine their authority. Others may simply be uncomfortable with the idea of relying on data to make decisions. To overcome this resistance, organizations need to focus on changing management strategies that emphasize the value of data-driven decision-making. This might involve highlighting case studies of successful data-driven initiatives, providing training to build confidence in data usage, and creating incentives for employees who embrace data in their roles. Leaders play a critical role in this process by modeling data-driven behaviors and demonstrating the positive impact of using data in decision-making.

2. Siloed Data and Technology Constraints: Technical limitations, such as siloed data and outdated systems, can also hinder the development of a data-driven culture. When data is difficult to access or spread across multiple platforms, it becomes challenging for employees to use it effectively in their work. To address this issue, companies need to invest in modern data infrastructure that promotes data integration, sharing, and accessibility. This might involve implementing cloud-based data platforms, adopting data visualization tools that make it easier to analyze and interpret data, and ensuring that data governance policies are in place to maintain data quality and security.

3. Leadership Buy-In: While leadership commitment is essential to building a data-driven culture, securing buy-in from executives can sometimes be a challenge. Leaders who are not familiar with data science may be skeptical of its value or uncertain about how to integrate it into their decision-making processes. To build leadership buy-in, data scientists and analysts need to focus on demonstrating the tangible benefits of data-driven decision-making. This could involve presenting data-backed case studies that show how data has improved business outcomes or creating pilot projects that highlight the potential impact of using data to solve specific challenges. By building a strong business case for data, organizations can secure the support of key decision-makers.

Building a Data-Driven Culture at Google

Google is often cited as a prime example of a company with a deeply ingrained data-driven culture. At Google, data is at the heart of everything from product development to talent management. The company's data-driven approach is evident in how it makes decisions, evaluates employee performance, and develops new products and services.

One of the key factors behind Google's success in building a data-driven culture is its commitment to experimentation and measurement. The company encourages employees to test new ideas and relies heavily on A/B testing to evaluate the impact of changes in its products and services. This culture of experimentation is supported by a robust data infrastructure that allows employees to access the information they need to make informed decisions quickly. In addition to fostering a culture of experimentation, Google places a strong emphasis on data transparency. Employees have access to vast amounts of data, and the company's internal tools make it easy for teams to collaborate on data projects. This openness and accessibility help ensure that data is integrated into every aspect of the business.

Building a data-driven culture is a long-term effort that requires commitment from leadership, investment in data infrastructure, and a focus on employee engagement and education. By creating an environment where data is accessible, understood, and valued by everyone, organizations can unlock the full potential of their data and use it to drive innovation, improve decision-making, and gain a competitive advantage. In the next chapters, we will explore how data scientists can align their projects with business strategy, collaborate effectively across departments, and overcome common challenges in implementing data-driven initiatives. But it all begins with culture—creating the foundation for a data-driven organization that uses data to shape its future.

CHAPTER 5

Aligning Data Initiatives with Business Strategy

Data science has the potential to be one of the most valuable assets for any organization, but for that value to be fully realized, data initiatives must be closely aligned with the overarching business strategy. Too often, data projects are undertaken in isolation, driven by curiosity or technological capabilities rather than by strategic business goals. While such projects may yield interesting insights, they fail to have a significant impact if they don't connect to the company's larger objectives. In this chapter, we will explore how data scientists can ensure their work is directly contributing to the organization's success by aligning data initiatives with business strategy. We will dive into the importance of understanding the business' vision and goals, the frameworks data scientists can use to map their projects to these goals, and how to ensure continuous alignment through ongoing collaboration with leadership and other departments.

The Importance of Strategic Alignment

At its core, aligning data initiatives with business strategy means ensuring that every data-driven effort is aimed at solving a business problem or enhancing an aspect of the company's performance. This requires a deep understanding of both the technical side of data science and the business side of the organization. Data scientists who can master this dual perspective are not only more likely to see their projects implemented but also have a greater impact on the company's success. The most successful data projects are those that address a clear business need. For example, consider a company struggling with customer churn. A well-aligned data initiative might involve building predictive models to identify at-risk customers and recommend retention strategies. In this case, the data project directly supports the company's strategic goal of reducing churn and increasing customer retention. On the other hand, a misaligned data project—one that focuses on an isolated problem or exploratory analysis without a clear connection to business goals—may provide interesting insights but ultimately fail to influence the company's decision-making. Without strategic alignment, even the most sophisticated data analyses can be overlooked by decision-makers who are focused on immediate business priorities. Aligning data initiatives with business strategy ensures that data scientists are not just solving technical problems but are contributing to the overall growth, efficiency, and success of the business. This alignment also makes it easier for data scientists to secure buy-in from leadership, as executives are more likely to support projects that clearly address their top priorities.

Understanding Business Goals and Objectives

To align data initiatives with business strategy, data scientists must first have a thorough understanding of the company's goals, both short-term and long-term. These goals are typically outlined in the company's business plan, mission statement, or strategic roadmaps. Business goals can vary widely depending on the industry, market conditions, and company stage, but they generally fall into categories such as revenue growth, cost reduction, market expansion, product development, and customer satisfaction.

Types of Business Goals:

Revenue Growth: Many companies prioritize increasing revenue as a key business goal. Data initiatives that support revenue growth might involve identifying new customer segments, optimizing pricing strategies, or improving the effectiveness of marketing campaigns through predictive analytics.

Cost Reduction: In some cases, reducing operational costs is the primary focus. Data projects aligned with this goal could include improving supply chain efficiency, minimizing waste in production processes, or automating routine tasks using machine learning algorithms.

Customer Retention and Satisfaction: For businesses that rely heavily on recurring revenue or customer loyalty, retaining customers and improving customer satisfaction are often top strategic priorities. Data scientists can align their projects with these goals by analyzing customer behavior, predicting churn, or designing personalized recommendations to improve the customer experience.

Market Expansion: Companies looking to expand into new markets may benefit from data initiatives that provide insights into market trends, customer preferences, and competitive dynamics. Predictive models and advanced analytics can help identify the best opportunities for market entry or expansion.

To gain a deep understanding of the company's goals, data scientists should regularly collaborate with business leaders. This might involve attending strategic planning meetings, reviewing the company's performance metrics, and engaging in discussions with executives to learn about their pain points and priorities. By staying informed about the company's strategic direction, data scientists can ensure their work remains relevant and aligned with business needs. Additionally, collaboration with business leaders provides data scientists with the opportunity to educate decision-makers about the potential of data science. Many executives are eager to embrace data-driven strategies but may not fully understand how data science can contribute to their goals. By bridging this knowledge gap, data scientists can build stronger relationships with leadership and ensure that data initiatives are viewed as critical to the company's success.

Frameworks for Strategic Alignment

To effectively align data projects with business strategy, data scientists need a structured approach that helps them map their initiatives to business goals. Several frameworks can be used to achieve this alignment, including Objectives and Key Results (OKRs), the Balanced Scorecard, and value stream mapping.

1. Objectives and Key Results (OKRs): The OKR framework is widely used by companies to set and track business objectives and their associated outcomes. OKRs consist of high-level objectives (what the organization wants to achieve) and key results (the specific, measurable outcomes that indicate progress toward the objective). For data scientists, OKRs offer a clear way to align their projects with business goals. For example, if the company's objective is to increase customer retention, a data scientist's OKR might develop a churn prediction model with a key result of reducing churn by 10% over the next quarter. This approach provides a direct link between the data initiative and the company's strategic goals, making it easier to measure the impact of the data project. OKRs also encourage collaboration across departments, as different teams are often responsible for contributing to the same key results. This cross-functional alignment ensures that data projects are integrated into the company's overall efforts to achieve its strategic objectives.

2. The Balanced Scorecard: The Balanced Scorecard is another popular framework used to align business activities with strategic goals. It measures performance across four key areas: financial performance, customer satisfaction, internal processes, and innovation/growth. Data scientists can use the Balanced Scorecard to identify which area their work supports and align their projects accordingly. For example, if a company is focused on improving customer satisfaction, data scientists might work on developing sentiment analysis models to analyze customer feedback or use predictive analytics to personalize the customer experience. Similarly, if the focus is on internal processes, data projects could involve optimizing workflows or identifying bottlenecks in the production process. The Balanced Scorecard provides a holistic view of the company's performance, allowing data scientists to ensure their work contributes to multiple areas of the business, not just financial outcomes.

3. Value Stream Mapping: Value stream mapping is a Lean management technique that helps organizations visualize the flow of materials, information, and activities required to deliver a product or service to the customer. For data scientists, value stream mapping can be a useful tool for identifying where data-driven insights can add the most value in the business process. By analyzing the company's value streams, data scientists can identify inefficiencies, redundancies, or areas where data could enhance decision-making. For example, in a manufacturing company, value stream mapping might reveal that delays in the supply chain are causing production bottlenecks. A data-driven initiative focused on improving supply chain forecasting could help resolve these issues, contributing directly to the company's strategic goal of increasing operational efficiency.

Ensuring Continuous Alignment

Aligning data initiatives with business strategy is not a one-time exercise, it requires ongoing collaboration and adjustment as business priorities evolve. To ensure continuous alignment, data scientists must maintain regular communication with leadership, stay informed about changes in the company's strategic direction, and be proactive in suggesting new data-driven initiatives.

Regular Check-Ins with Leadership: One of the most effective ways to ensure continuous alignment is through regular check-ins with business leaders. These meetings provide an opportunity for data scientists to present their progress, share insights, and discuss how their work is contributing to the company's goals. It also allows leadership to provide feedback and adjust priorities based on changing market conditions or new business opportunities. Regular check-ins ensure that data projects remain relevant and aligned with the company's evolving strategy. It also fosters a collaborative relationship between data scientists and executives, increasing the likelihood that data-driven initiatives will be supported and implemented.

Agility in Data Projects: Business strategies are not static, they evolve in response to market shifts, competitive pressures, and internal developments. Data scientists must be agile in their approach, ready to pivot their projects when business priorities change. This might involve shifting focus from one area of the business to another or adjusting the scope of a project to meet new strategic objectives. For example, a data initiative focused on market expansion might need to pivot if the company decides to prioritize customer retention due to economic uncertainty. By staying flexible and responsive to changing business needs, data scientists can ensure their work remains aligned with the company's most pressing goals.

Cross-Functional Collaboration: Data initiatives often require input and collaboration from multiple departments, including marketing, finance, operations, and product development. Ensuring that data projects are aligned with business strategy requires close collaboration with these teams, as they provide valuable context and expertise that can help guide the direction of data projects. Cross-functional collaboration also ensures that data insights are implemented effectively. For example, if a data scientist develops a predictive model to improve customer retention, the marketing and customer service teams will need to work together to act on the insights and implement the recommended strategies. By fostering a culture of collaboration, data scientists can ensure their work has a tangible impact on the business.

Measuring the Success of Data Initiatives

To demonstrate the value of aligning data initiatives with business strategy, it's important to measure the success of data projects in terms that matter to the organization. This typically involves tracking the key metrics and outcomes that are tied to the company's strategic goals.

Key Performance Indicators (KPIs): KPIs are the metrics that leadership uses to measure progress toward strategic objectives. Data scientists should ensure that their projects are directly linked to relevant KPIs. For example, if the company's goal is to increase revenue, the relevant KPI might be sales growth. If the goal is to reduce operational costs, the KPI might be cost per unit produced. By tracking KPIs, data scientists can provide clear evidence of the impact of their work. This not only helps justify the resources allocated to data initiatives but also builds trust with leadership, as the results of data projects are directly tied to measurable business outcomes.

Quantifying the Business Impact: In addition to tracking KPIs, data scientists should quantify the business impact of their projects wherever possible. This might involve calculating the financial savings generated by a cost-reduction initiative, estimating the revenue uplift from a customer segmentation model, or projecting the potential ROI of a new market expansion strategy. By providing concrete evidence of the value created by data initiatives, data scientists can demonstrate the strategic importance of their work and ensure continued support from leadership.

Aligning Data Initiatives at Netflix

Netflix is widely regarded as one of the most data-driven companies in the world. On Netflix, data is used not only to optimize the user experience through personalized recommendations but also to inform strategic decisions related to content production, market expansion, and customer retention. One of the key ways Netflix aligns its data initiatives with business strategy is through its use of predictive analytics to guide content investment decisions. Rather than relying on intuition or traditional market research, Netflix uses data-driven insights to identify what types of content will resonate with its audience. This approach has allowed Netflix to create hit shows like Stranger Things and The Crown, which were developed based on data about viewer preferences. Netflix's data team works closely with leadership to ensure that data initiatives are aligned with the company's overall growth strategy. By using data to inform content decisions, optimize user engagement, and reduce churn, Netflix has been able to maintain its position as a leader in the highly competitive streaming industry. Aligning data initiatives with business strategy is critical for ensuring that data-driven insights translate into real business outcomes. By understanding the company's goals, using frameworks like OKRs and the Balanced Scorecard, and maintaining ongoing collaboration with leadership, data scientists can ensure their work is strategically relevant and impactful. As we move into the next chapters, we'll explore how data scientists can foster collaboration across teams, overcome challenges in data-driven decision-making, and use advanced analytics to support long-term strategic planning. But at the heart of all these efforts is the need for alignment—ensuring that every data project is aimed at solving a business problem and contributing to the company's success.

CHAPTER 6

Translating Data Insights into Actionable Business Strategies

Data science is about more than discovering patterns or building predictive models—it's about transforming data into insights that drive meaningful business decisions. However, the real value of data insights lies not in the analysis itself, but in how those insights are applied to solve business problems, improve operations, and enhance competitive advantage. In this chapter, we will explore the process of translating data insights into actionable business strategies, a crucial skill for any data scientist aiming to have a strategic impact within an organization. We will dive into methods for framing insights in a business context, techniques for creating actionable recommendations from data, and the role of communication in ensuring that data insights are understood and implemented by decision-makers.

The Journey from Data to Action

For many data scientists, the challenge isn't in generating insights—it's in translating those insights into actions that align with business goals. A model may reveal a predictive pattern, or an analysis may uncover a previously unseen trend, but unless those findings can be connected to business outcomes, their value remains untapped.

Understanding the Business Context: The first step in translating data insights into business strategies is understanding the business context in which those insights will be applied. Data scientists must not only be aware of the technical details of their analyses but also grasp the broader business landscape, including the company's objectives, market conditions, and operational challenges. For example, imagine a data scientist working in a retail company. Their analysis of customer data might reveal that customers who purchase a particular product category are more likely to make repeat purchases within six months. While this insight is valuable, its true business value depends on the company's current goals. If the company is focused on improving customer retention, this insight can be used to design targeted loyalty programs or marketing campaigns aimed at those repeat customers. However, if the company's primary goal is cost reduction, the same insight might lead to a different action—perhaps optimizing inventory levels for that product category to minimize carrying costs.

From Insight to Strategy: To move from insight to strategy, data scientists need to ask a critical question: How can this insight be used to improve the business? This involves thinking beyond the data itself and considering the practical implications of the findings. For example, a machine learning model might predict that certain customers are at a high risk of churn. While this is a valuable insight, the strategy comes from determining how to act on that information. Should the company offer at-risk customers discounts? Should it improve customer service for these individuals? Or should it focus on developing new features to keep them engaged? Data scientists must work closely with business leaders to identify the best course of action based on the data. The process of translating insights into strategies requires an understanding of both the technical aspects of data science and the strategic priorities of the business. Data scientists need to frame their recommendations in a way that speaks to business objectives, whether it's improving customer satisfaction, increasing revenue, or optimizing operations.

Framing Insights into a Business Context

One of the key challenges in translating data insights into business strategies is framing those insights in a way that resonates with non-technical stakeholders. Business leaders are often more interested in the outcomes and implications of data than in the technical details behind the analysis. As a result, data scientists must be able to communicate their findings in a way that emphasizes business value rather than technical complexity.

Focus on Business Outcomes: When presenting data insights, it's important to focus on the outcomes that are most relevant to the business. For example, instead of explaining the technical workings of a predictive model, data scientists should emphasize how the model can be used to increase sales, reduce churn, or improve customer engagement. This involves translating technical metrics (e.g., accuracy, precision, recall) into business metrics (e.g., revenue growth, customer retention rate, operational efficiency). For instance, a data scientist working for an e-commerce company might build a model that predicts customer behavior based on past purchases. Rather than focusing on the model's performance metrics, the data scientist should present the key takeaway: *"Our model predicts that customers who buy Product A are 30% more likely to make a second purchase within three months. By offering targeted promotions to these customers, we could increase our repeat purchase rate by 10%, potentially adding $1 million in revenue over the next year.* By focusing on business outcomes, data scientists can ensure that their insights are understood and valued by decision-makers, increasing the likelihood that their recommendations will be implemented.

Using the Right Language: In addition to focusing on business outcomes, data scientists need to use language that resonates with business leaders. This means avoiding overly technical jargon and instead framing insights in terms of risk, opportunity, and value creation. For example, rather than explaining a decision tree algorithm, a data scientist might say: *"We've identified a clear* *pattern in customer behavior that suggests certain groups are more likely to respond to specific marketing messages. By tailoring our campaigns to these groups, we can improve conversion rates and reduce marketing costs.* By framing insights in the language of business, data scientists can bridge the gap between technical analysis and strategic decision-making.

Making Insights Actionable: To ensure that data insights lead to action, data scientists must go beyond presenting findings—they must provide clear recommendations on what the business should do next. This involves thinking through the practical steps that the company can take based on the data and providing guidance on how to implement those steps. For example, if an analysis shows that customer churn is increasing, the actionable insight might be to implement a customer retention program targeting high-risk customers. The data scientist could recommend specific actions, such as offering discounts or personalized support, and provide estimates of the potential impact of these initiatives. By making insights actionable, data scientists can ensure that their work doesn't stop at the analysis phase but instead drives real business outcomes.

Building a Strategy from Data Insights

Once data insights have been framed in a business context, the next step is to build a strategy around those insights. This involves identifying the key actions that should be taken based on the data and developing a plan for implementing those actions.

Identifying Key Actions: The first step in building a strategy from data insights is identifying the key actions that the company should take. This requires collaboration between data scientists and business leaders to determine the best course of action based on the data. For example, if a retail company's data shows that a certain product category is driving repeat purchases, the key actions might include increasing inventory for that category, launching targeted marketing campaigns to promote the product, and optimizing pricing strategies to maximize profit margins. By working closely with business leaders, data scientists can ensure that the actions identified are aligned with the company's strategic goals and have the potential to deliver measurable results.

Creating a Plan for Implementation: Once the key actions have been identified, the next step is to create a plan for implementing those actions. This involves determining who will be responsible for executing the plan, setting timelines for implementation, and establishing metrics to measure success. For example, in the case of a customer retention strategy, the marketing team might be responsible for designing and executing targeted campaigns, while the customer service team might be tasked with improving support for at-risk customers. The data scientist's role might include providing ongoing analysis to track the effectiveness of these initiatives and adjusting the strategy as needed. By creating a clear plan for implementation, data scientists can ensure that their insights lead to tangible results and that the business has a roadmap for achieving its goals.

Tracking and Measuring Success: To ensure that the strategy is working, it's important to establish metrics for tracking success. These metrics should be tied to the company's strategic goals and provide a clear indication of whether the actions taken are having the desired impact. For example, if the goal is to reduce customer churn, the key metrics might include the churn rate, customer retention rate, and customer satisfaction scores. If the goal is to increase revenue, the metrics might include sales growth, average order value, and conversion rates. By tracking these metrics, data scientists and business leaders can monitor the success of the strategy and make adjustments as needed to improve performance.

Communicating Data-Driven Strategies to Stakeholders

Once a data-driven strategy has been developed, it's important to communicate that strategy to all relevant stakeholders. This ensures that everyone involved in the implementation process understands the goals, actions, and expected outcomes of the strategy.

Engaging Business Leaders: The first step in communicating a data-driven strategy is engaging business leaders. Data scientists must present their findings in a way that resonates with executives and highlights the strategic value of the proposed actions. For example, in a presentation to the executive team, a data scientist might explain how a new pricing strategy, based on predictive analytics, could increase revenue by 15% over the next year. The presentation should focus on the business impact of the strategy and provide clear, actionable recommendations for implementation. By engaging business leaders early in the process, data scientists can secure buy-in for their strategy and ensure that it has the support needed for successful implementation.

Collaborating with Cross-Functional Teams: In many cases, implementing a data-driven strategy requires collaboration across multiple departments, including marketing, sales, operations, and customer service. Data scientists must communicate the strategy to these teams and work with them to ensure that the necessary actions are taken. For example, if a data-driven strategy involves optimizing the supply chain to reduce costs, the data scientist might work closely with the operations team to analyze current processes, identify inefficiencies, and implement data-driven improvements. Collaboration is key to ensuring that data insights are translated into action across the organization. By working closely with cross-functional teams, data scientists can ensure that their strategy is implemented effectively and delivers the desired results.

Continuous Communication and Feedback: Communication doesn't end once the strategy has been implemented. To ensure ongoing success, data scientists should maintain regular communication with stakeholders, providing updates on the progress of the strategy and making adjustments as needed. For example, if a data-driven marketing campaign is underperforming, the data scientist might analyze the results and recommend changes to improve its effectiveness. By providing continuous feedback and adjusting the strategy based on new data, data scientists can ensure that the strategy remains aligned with business goals and continues to deliver value.

Data-Driven Strategy at Spotify

Spotify is a prime example of a company that has successfully translated data insights into actionable business strategies. One of Spotify's key challenges is retaining its large and diverse user base in a highly competitive market. To address this challenge, Spotify relies heavily on data-driven strategies to personalize the user experience and keep users engaged. Using data on user behavior, Spotify has developed sophisticated recommendation algorithms that suggest songs, playlists, and podcasts tailored to individual preferences. These recommendations are based on insights derived from listening habits, likes, and user interactions with the platform. By translating these insights into personalized recommendations, Spotify has been able to increase user engagement and reduce churn, contributing to its long-term growth strategy. Spotify's data-driven approach doesn't stop at recommendations. The company also uses data to inform its content acquisition strategy, helping it identify emerging music trends and invest in the right artists and genres. By aligning its data initiatives with its business goals, Spotify has successfully translated data insights into strategies that drive user retention, content development, and overall business growth. Translating data insights into actionable business strategies is the key to ensuring that data science delivers real value to the organization. By understanding the business context, framing insights in a way that resonates with decision-makers, and building clear, actionable strategies, data scientists can bridge the gap between analysis and action. As we move forward in this book, we will explore the challenges that arise in implementing data-driven strategies, including cross-functional collaboration, data governance, and overcoming resistance to change. But at the heart of every successful data initiative is the ability to turn insights into impact—using data not just to inform decisions, but to drive meaningful business outcomes.

CHAPTER 7

Advanced Analytics and AI in Strategic Decision-Making

As organizations seek to remain competitive in an increasingly data-driven world, the role of advanced analytics and artificial intelligence (AI) in business strategy has become more prominent. Leveraging the power of machine learning, predictive modeling, and AI, businesses can not only analyze past data but also anticipate future trends, automate decision-making processes, and enhance operational efficiency. This chapter explores the growing role of advanced analytics and AI in strategic decision-making, highlighting how these tools can provide a competitive edge and transform the way businesses operate. We will cover the different types of advanced analytics, delve into AI applications in business, examine the use of predictive and prescriptive analytics, and explore the ethical considerations and risks involved in using AI for decision-making. Through real-world examples and case studies, we will also illustrate how companies are already using advanced analytics and AI to drive their strategies forward.

The Rise of Advanced Analytics in Business

Advanced analytics refers to a set of techniques and tools that go beyond traditional data analysis to predict future outcomes, optimize business processes, and provide more granular insights into complex problems. It encompasses a wide range of methods, including machine learning, natural language processing, predictive modeling, and AI. The goal of advanced analytics is not just to understand what has happened in the past but to predict future trends, identify patterns, and generate recommendations for strategic actions.

Types of Advanced Analytics:

Descriptive Analytics: This form of analytics focuses on summarizing historical data to answer the question, "What happened?" It involves aggregating and analyzing data to provide insights into past performance, such as sales trends, customer behavior, or operational efficiency.

Diagnostic Analytics: Going beyond descriptive analytics, diagnostic analytics seeks to answer the question, "Why did it happen?" This involves deeper analysis to uncover the underlying causes of specific outcomes. Techniques such as data mining and correlation analysis are often used in this stage.

Predictive Analytics: Predictive analytics involves using historical data to make predictions about future events. Machine learning models and statistical techniques are employed to forecast outcomes such as customer behavior, market trends, or potential risks. The key question here is, "What is likely to happen?"

Prescriptive Analytics: Prescriptive analytics is the most advanced form of analytics, as it not only predicts future outcomes but also recommends actions based on those predictions. This form of analytics helps businesses decide the best course of action to optimize outcomes, reduce risk, and capitalize on opportunities. The core question is, "What should we do about it?"

Artificial Intelligence in Business Strategy

AI is transforming how businesses operate by automating processes, enhancing decision-making, and enabling personalized customer experiences. AI systems use algorithms that learn from data to make predictions, automate tasks, and generate insights, often in real time. AI's role in strategic decision-making is growing, as it allows businesses to leverage vast amounts of data and make more informed, accurate, and timely decisions.

Key AI Applications in Business:

Automation of Repetitive Tasks: One of the most widespread applications of AI in business is the automation of routine, repetitive tasks. AI-powered systems can handle customer inquiries, manage inventory, or process transactions with little to no human intervention. This allows businesses to reduce costs and allocate human resources to more strategic, high-value tasks.

Predictive Maintenance: In industries such as manufacturing, AI is being used to predict equipment failures before they happen. By analyzing sensor data and operational history, AI systems can forecast when a machine is likely to fail and recommend preventive maintenance. This minimizes downtime and reduces the costs associated with unexpected breakdowns.

Customer Personalization: AI-driven recommendation engines, such as those used by Amazon or Netflix, analyze user behavior to make personalized product or content recommendations. These systems enhance customer satisfaction, improve engagement, and drive revenue by delivering personalized experiences on a scale.

AI in Sales and Marketing: AI is increasingly being used in sales and marketing to optimize campaigns, identify high-potential leads, and personalize customer interactions. For example, AI can analyze customer data to predict which leads are most likely to convert, allowing sales teams to focus their efforts more effectively. AI can also optimize marketing spending by identifying which channels and messages resonate best with target audiences.

Risk Management and Fraud Detection: In finance and banking, AI is being used to detect fraud, assess credit risk, and improve regulatory compliance. Machine learning models analyze transaction data to identify suspicious activity in real-time, flagging potential fraud cases before they escalate. AI-powered risk management systems also help financial institutions make better lending decisions by analyzing a broader set of data points, including alternative data sources such as social media activity.

Predictive and Prescriptive Analytics in Decision-Making

While descriptive and diagnostic analytics help organizations understand the past, predictive and prescriptive analytics offer the ability to anticipate the future and take proactive actions. These two forms of analytics are becoming increasingly important in strategic decision-making, providing businesses with the insights needed to stay ahead of the competition.

Predictive Analytics: Predictive analytics uses historical data to forecast future outcomes, enabling organizations to anticipate customer behavior, market trends, and operational risks. Predictive models use machine learning algorithms to analyze patterns in data, allowing businesses to make informed decisions based on probabilities. For example, a retail company might use predictive analytics to forecast sales for the next quarter. By analyzing historical sales data, customer demographics, and seasonal trends, the company can anticipate demand for specific products and adjust its inventory accordingly. Similarly, a telecommunications company might use predictive analytics to identify customers at risk of churning and develop targeted retention strategies to prevent them from leaving.

Prescriptive Analytics: While predictive analytics forecasts what is likely to happen, prescriptive analytics goes a step further by recommending specific actions to optimize outcomes. Prescriptive analytics combines predictive models with optimization algorithms to provide recommendations on the best course of action. For example, an airline might use prescriptive analytics to determine the optimal pricing strategy for flights. By analyzing historical ticket sales, competitor pricing, and market demand, the airline can identify the price points that maximize revenue while maintaining occupancy rates. Similarly, a manufacturing company might use prescriptive analytics to optimize its production schedule, minimizing downtime and reducing costs.

AI in Strategic Decision-Making: Real-World Applications

AI's impact on business strategy is evident across industries, with companies using AI to enhance decision-making, improve efficiency, and gain a competitive edge. The following case studies highlight how AI is being applied to drive strategic decision-making.

Case Study 1: AI in Retail – Walmart, one of the world's largest retailers, has embraced AI to optimize its supply chain and improve inventory management. By using machine learning algorithms to analyze vast amounts of data, Walmart can predict demand for specific products at different store locations. This enables the company to adjust its inventory levels in real time, ensuring that shelves are stocked with the right products at the right time. Walmart also uses AI to optimize its pricing strategy. By analyzing competitor prices, sales data, and customer behavior, the company can dynamically adjust its prices to remain competitive while maximizing profits. These AI-driven strategies have helped Walmart reduce costs, improve customer satisfaction, and maintain its position as a market leader.

Case Study 2: AI in Finance – JPMorgan Chase JPMorgan Chase has been a pioneer in using AI for fraud detection and risk management. The bank's AI-powered systems analyze billions of transactions in real-time to identify suspicious activity and prevent fraudulent transactions. By using machine learning algorithms, the bank can detect patterns of fraud that would be impossible for humans to identify manually. In addition to fraud detection, JPMorgan Chase uses AI to optimize its investment strategies. The bank's AI systems analyze market data, economic indicators, and historical trends to provide recommendations for portfolio management. These AI-driven insights enable the bank to make more informed investment decisions and improve returns for its clients.

Case Study 3: AI in Healthcare – IBM Watson Health IBM Watson Health has leveraged AI to revolutionize healthcare by improving diagnosis, treatment, and patient care. Watson's AI capabilities allow it to analyze vast amounts of medical data, including patient records, clinical trials, and research papers, to provide doctors with evidence-based recommendations for treatment. For example, Watson can analyze a patient's medical history and recommend personalized treatment plans based on the latest research and clinical guidelines. This helps doctors make more informed decisions and improves patient outcomes. AI's ability to process and analyze medical data at scale has the potential to transform healthcare, making treatments more effective and accessible.

Leveraging AI and Advanced Analytics for Strategic Success

Advanced analytics and AI have the potential to revolutionize the way businesses make decisions, providing insights that go beyond traditional data analysis and enabling organizations to anticipate future trends, optimize operations, and drive growth. By incorporating predictive and prescriptive analytics into their decision-making processes, businesses can develop proactive strategies that address challenges before they arise and capitalize on emerging opportunities. However, as with any powerful technology, the use of AI and advanced analytics comes with ethical considerations and risks. Businesses must be mindful of issues such as bias, privacy, and job displacement, ensuring that their AI systems are designed and implemented in a way that promotes fairness, transparency, and accountability. As we move forward in this book, we will explore the practical challenges of integrating advanced analytics and AI into business strategy, from building cross-functional teams to ensuring data governance and overcoming resistance to change. But the potential for AI and advanced analytics to transform business strategies is undeniable, and organizations that embrace these technologies will be well-positioned to lead in the data-driven future.

CHAPTER 8

Cross-Functional Collaboration: Partnering with Business and Technology Teams

I n today's data-driven world, one of the most critical factors for successfully implementing data initiatives is effective cross-functional collaboration. Data scientists cannot work in isolation; to drive meaningful business outcomes, they must collaborate closely with various teams across the organization, including business leaders, marketing, sales, operations, product development, and IT. This collaboration ensures that data insights are properly understood, prioritized, and implemented in ways that directly impact the company's goals. This chapter delves into the importance of cross-functional collaboration, exploring the roles of different departments, how data teams can work seamlessly with business and technology teams, and the challenges of fostering collaboration in siloed environments. By building strong partnerships across departments, data scientists can ensure that their insights are not only relevant but also actionable and aligned with the organization's strategic goals.

The Need for Cross-Functional Collaboration in Data Initiatives

The complexity of modern businesses means that data is often scattered across various departments, systems, and teams. To unlock the full value of this data, data scientists need input from multiple areas of the business. Whether it's gathering domain knowledge from marketing, understanding operational constraints from the supply chain team, or working with IT to ensure data availability, collaboration is key to creating insights that are both accurate and actionable.

Why Cross-Functional Collaboration is Critical: Data initiatives don't exist in a vacuum; they must be integrated into the business's broader goals to create real impact. Cross-functional collaboration ensures that data projects are aligned with the needs of the business and are prioritized appropriately. It also allows data scientists to:

Gain a better understanding of the business context in which the data is being used.

Ensure that data insights are directly relevant to the challenges that other teams are facing.

Facilitate smoother implementation of data-driven recommendations by working closely with the teams responsible for executing them.

For example, a data team might develop a predictive model that forecasts customer churn. However, if they don't collaborate with the marketing or customer service departments, they may miss critical details about customer touchpoints, campaign timings, or service-related factors that influence churn. By collaborating across functions, data teams can create models that are more accurate and more likely to drive actionable recommendations.

Overcoming Siloed Structures: Many organizations operate with a traditional siloed structure, where different departments work independently from one another, each with its own goals, priorities, and data. While this structure can create efficiencies within departments, it also creates barriers to collaboration, particularly when it comes to data initiatives. Silos prevent the free flow of information, making it difficult for data scientists to access the data they need and hindering efforts to align data projects with business goals. To overcome these silos, organizations must foster a culture of collaboration, where teams are encouraged to share data, ideas, and insights.

Key Departments in Cross-Functional Collaboration

Effective cross-functional collaboration requires input from multiple departments, each of which plays a unique role in ensuring that data insights lead to actionable outcomes. Below, we explore the key departments that data scientists typically collaborate with and the roles they play in data initiatives.

1. Marketing and Sales Teams: Marketing and sales teams are often on the front lines of customer interaction, making them critical partners in data-driven initiatives aimed at improving customer engagement, targeting, and conversion rates.

Marketing: Data scientists can collaborate with marketing teams to analyze customer behavior, segment audiences, and optimize campaigns. Predictive models can identify which customer segments are most likely to respond to certain marketing efforts, while data-driven insights can help tailor messaging and offers to maximize engagement and sales.

Sales: Sales teams benefit from data insights that help prioritize leads, optimize sales processes, and improve customer retention. Predictive models can identify high-potential leads, allowing sales teams to focus their efforts where they are most likely to succeed. Data scientists can also help sales teams analyze performance metrics, identify trends, and adjust strategies accordingly.

For example, a marketing team might need insights into the best time to launch a campaign or the customer segments that are most likely to engage with a new product. The data team can provide historical data analysis, predictive insights, and A/B testing results to guide campaign planning.

2. Product Development and Operations: Data scientists often collaborate with product development and operations teams to drive product innovation and operational efficiency. These teams rely on data insights to make decisions about product features, inventory management, and process optimization.

Product Development: In product development, data insights are essential for understanding customer needs, usage patterns, and pain points. By analyzing customer feedback, user behavior, and market trends, data scientists can help product teams identify which features are most likely to resonate with users and where improvements are needed.

Operations: Data insights are also critical for optimizing operational processes. In manufacturing, supply chain, and logistics, data-driven models can be used to forecast demand, optimize inventory levels, and streamline production schedules. Collaboration between data scientists and operations teams ensures that these models take into account real-world constraints, such as supply chain disruptions or capacity limitations.

For instance, an operations team might need to optimize the supply chain to reduce costs. The data team can use historical data and machine learning algorithms to predict demand and recommend adjustments to inventory levels or distribution schedules.

3. Finance and Risk Management: Collaboration with finance and risk management teams allows data scientists to develop models that support financial forecasting, budgeting, and risk analysis.

Finance: Finance teams rely on data to develop accurate financial forecasts, optimize budgets, and analyze the profitability of different business units. Data scientists can contribute by building models that forecast revenue, assess the financial impact of new initiatives, and identify cost-saving opportunities.

Risk Management: In industries such as finance, insurance, and healthcare, risk management teams work closely with data scientists to identify potential risks and develop mitigation strategies. Predictive analytics can be used to assess credit risk, detect fraud, or anticipate operational risks.

For example, in a financial institution, data scientists might collaborate with the risk management team to build models that detect fraudulent transactions or assess creditworthiness. By working together, they can ensure that the models are accurate, reliable, and aligned with regulatory requirements.

4. IT and Data Engineering Teams: Collaboration between data scientists and IT or data engineering teams is essential for ensuring data accessibility, quality, and security. These teams are responsible for maintaining the company's data infrastructure, which includes data storage, processing, and governance.

Data Engineering: Data engineers work to ensure that data is properly collected, cleaned, and organized, making it accessible for analysis. Collaboration with data engineers allows data scientists to access high-quality data and ensures that data pipelines are optimized for efficient processing.

IT: IT teams play a crucial role in implementing data security measures, ensuring compliance with data privacy regulations, and providing the infrastructure needed for running advanced analytics and machine learning models. Collaboration between data scientists and IT teams ensures that data projects are both secure and scalable.

For example, a data scientist might need access to customer data from multiple systems, such as the CRM, ERP, and online sales platforms. The IT and data engineering teams can collaborate to ensure that the data is integrated and accessible through a centralized data platform, enabling the data scientist to perform more comprehensive analyses.

Best Practices for Fostering Collaboration

Fostering effective cross-functional collaboration requires more than simply encouraging teams to work together. Organizations must create a culture that values collaboration and provide the tools and processes needed to facilitate it. Below are some best practices for fostering collaboration between data teams and other departments.

1. Establish Clear Communication Channels: Clear and open communication is essential for effective collaboration. Organizations should establish formal communication channels, such as regular cross-departmental meetings or collaborative platforms like Slack or Microsoft Teams, where teams can share updates, discuss data insights, and ask questions. For example, a company might hold weekly meetings where data scientists, marketing teams, and product managers review data insights and discuss how they can be applied to upcoming campaigns or product development efforts.

2. Align Goals and Priorities: For collaboration to be effective, all teams involved must have a shared understanding of the organization's goals and priorities. Data scientists should work closely with business leaders to ensure that data projects are aligned with the company's strategic objectives. For instance, if the company's primary goal is to improve customer retention, the data team should focus its efforts on developing models that identify churn risks, while the marketing and customer service teams focus on implementing retention strategies. By aligning goals across departments, collaboration becomes more focused and results oriented.

3. Use Collaborative Tools: Collaborative tools, such as project management software, data visualization platforms, and shared dashboards, can make it easier for teams to collaborate on data projects. These tools provide a centralized location where teams can access data, track progress, and share insights. For example, a data team might use a tool like Tableau or Power BI to create interactive dashboards that allow marketing and sales teams to explore data in real-time, track key metrics, and make data-driven decisions without needing to rely on the data team for every report.

4. Foster a Culture of Data Literacy: One of the most common barriers to collaboration is a lack of data literacy among non-technical teams. To overcome this, organizations should invest in training and education to help employees develop the skills they need to work with data. By offering workshops, training sessions, and resources that teach employees how to interpret data, use data tools, and ask the right questions, organizations can foster a culture where data-driven decision-making is embraced across departments.

5. Empower Data Champions in Each Department: One effective way to promote collaboration is to identify "data champions" within each department—individuals who are both knowledgeable about data and passionate about its use in decision-making. These champions can serve as liaisons between their department and the data team, helping to bridge the gap between technical and non-technical teams. For example, a data champion in the marketing department might work closely with the data team to ensure that data-driven insights are incorporated into campaign strategies. They can also help train their colleagues in using data tools and interpreting analytics reports.

Overcoming Common Challenges in Collaboration

While cross-functional collaboration offers significant benefits, it is not without its challenges. Below are some of the most common obstacles to effective collaboration and strategies for overcoming them.

1. Lack of Data Accessibility: One of the most common challenges data teams faces is a lack of access to the data they need, often due to silos or technical barriers. To address this, organizations should invest in data integration and centralization tools that break down silos and ensure that data is accessible to all teams. By adopting cloud-based data platforms or creating centralized data lakes, organizations can ensure that data is easily accessible, enabling more seamless collaboration between departments.

2. Misalignment of Objectives: Misalignment between departmental objectives can hinder collaboration. For example, if the marketing team is focused on driving short-term sales, while the data team is working on long-term customer retention models, the two teams may struggle to find common ground. To overcome this, organizations should ensure that all departments are aligned with the company's overall strategic objectives. Regular strategy sessions, where leaders from each department collaborate to set shared goals and priorities, can help keep teams aligned and focused on the same outcomes.

3. Resistance to Change: In some cases, teams may resist adopting data-driven approaches, especially if they are used to making decisions based on intuition or experience. This resistance can hinder collaboration and limit the effectiveness of data initiatives. To overcome resistance, organizations should focus on building a culture that values data-driven decision-making. This can be achieved through leadership buy-in, training programs that emphasize the value of data, and clear demonstrations of how data insights can lead to better outcomes.

Cross-Functional Collaboration at Amazon

Amazon is a prime example of a company that has successfully implemented cross-functional collaboration to drive its data initiatives. With data at the core of its business model, Amazon's success is built on collaboration between data scientists, engineers, marketers, product managers, and supply chain teams. One of the ways Amazon fosters collaborations is through its use of shared dashboards and data visualization tools, which provide real-time access to key metrics for teams across the organization. These tools allow teams to monitor performance, track customer behavior, and make data-driven decisions without needing to rely on the data team for every insight. Amazon also promotes a culture of data literacy, ensuring that employees at all levels understand how to work with data and apply it to their decision-making processes. This has enabled the company to leverage data across all aspects of its operations, from optimizing its supply chain to personalizing customer experiences. By prioritizing cross-functional collaboration and investing in data accessibility, Amazon has built a culture where data is integrated into every decision, driving innovation and growth. Cross-functional collaboration is essential for the success of any data-driven initiative. By working closely with business, technology, and operations teams, data scientists can ensure that their insights are both actionable and aligned with the organization's strategic goals. Effective collaboration allows data teams to tap into the expertise of different departments, gain a deeper understanding of business challenges, and ensure that data insights lead to meaningful outcomes. As we move forward, the next chapters will explore the challenges of building a data-driven culture and overcoming barriers to aligning data initiatives with business goals. But at the heart of every successful data project is collaboration— ensuring that data scientists and business leaders work together to turn insights into action and drive organizational success.

CHAPTER 9

Overcoming Challenges in Aligning Data Science with Business

A s data becomes an increasingly valuable asset in organizations, the challenges of integrating data science into core business operations also grow. While companies understand the importance of data-driven decision-making, they often struggle to align their data science efforts with business goals. Misaligned priorities, organizational silos, resistance to change, and technical limitations are just a few of the obstacles that can prevent data initiatives from reaching their full potential. In this chapter, we will explore the most common challenges businesses face when trying to align data science with business strategy. We'll also look at practical solutions to overcome these challenges, drawing on real-world examples and case studies. By understanding these obstacles and how to address them, data scientists and business leaders can ensure that their data initiatives are driving real business value.

The Common Challenges in Aligning Data Science with Business Goals

Despite the tremendous potential of data science to improve decision-making, many organizations struggle to integrate data-driven approaches into their business strategies. Below are some of the most common challenges companies face when trying to align data science with business goals.

1. Lack of Business Understanding in Data Teams: One of the biggest challenges is the gap between data scientists and business leaders. Many data scientists come from technical or academic backgrounds and may lack a deep understanding of business processes, key performance indicators (KPIs), or the company's strategic priorities. This gap can lead to data projects that are interesting from a technical perspective but fail to address real business needs. For example, a data science team might focus on developing a complex machine learning model to predict customer behavior, but if they don't understand the specific goals of the marketing or sales teams, the model may not deliver actionable insights that align with the company's revenue or growth targets.

2. Misaligned Priorities Between Teams: Another common challenge is the misalignment of priorities between data teams and other departments. While the data team may be focused on exploring new technologies or building sophisticated models, business leaders may be more concerned with immediate issues such as improving customer retention, optimizing pricing, or reducing operational costs. This misalignment can result in data initiatives that don't resonate with business leaders, leading to a lack of support for data projects or failure to implement data-driven recommendations.

3. Organizational Silos and Data Fragmentation: Data fragmentation and siloed organizational structures are major barriers to aligning data science with business strategy. In many organizations, data is stored in separate systems across different departments, making it difficult for data scientists to access and analyze the full spectrum of data needed for comprehensive insights. For instance, customer data may be stored in a CRM system, while sales data is in an ERP system, and marketing data is scattered across various analytics tools. Without a unified data infrastructure, data scientists are unable to create a holistic view of the business, limiting their ability to generate insights that align with business goals.

4. Resistance to Data-Driven Decision-Making: Cultural resistance to data-driven decision-making is another significant obstacle. In some organizations, decision-makers may prefer to rely on intuition, experience, or legacy processes rather than trust data insights. This resistance can come from a lack of data literacy, fear of change, or skepticism about the accuracy and relevance of data models. Even when data scientists present valuable insights, resistance from key stakeholders can prevent those insights from being acted upon, rendering data projects ineffective.

5. Data Quality Issues: Poor data quality is a common issue that can derail data initiatives. If the data used for analysis is incomplete, outdated, or inaccurate, the insights generated will be flawed, leading to incorrect conclusions and potentially harmful business decisions. For example, a predictive model based on inaccurate customer data might provide misleading insights, causing a company to target the wrong customer segments or invest in ineffective marketing campaigns. Ensuring data quality is critical for aligning data science with business objectives.

6. Lack of Clear Communication: Effective communication between data scientists and business leaders is essential for aligning data initiatives with business strategy. However, data scientists often struggle to translate complex technical concepts into language that resonates with non-technical stakeholders. This communication gap can lead to misunderstandings, misaligned expectations, and a lack of support for data-driven initiatives. For instance, a data scientist might present a model's accuracy or precision metrics, but if these results aren't framed in terms of business impact (such as increased revenue or reduced churn), business leaders may not see the value in the project.

Solutions for Overcoming Alignment Challenges

While the challenges of aligning data science with business goals are significant, they are not insurmountable. Below are practical solutions for addressing these challenges and ensuring that data initiatives deliver real value to the organization.

1. Building Business Acumen in Data Teams: One of the most effective ways to align data science with business goals is to ensure that data scientists have a strong understanding of the business. This can be achieved through regular collaboration with business leaders, participation in strategic planning meetings, and targeted training programs focused on business fundamentals. By building business acumen within data teams, data scientists can better understand the company's objectives, KPIs, and operational challenges. This understanding allows them to develop data projects that are directly aligned with the company's goals, ensuring that their insights are relevant and actionable. For example, a data science team working for a retail company should have a solid understanding of the company's sales cycles, customer segmentation strategies, and revenue targets. This knowledge allows them to focus their efforts on projects that drive revenue growth, such as optimizing pricing strategies or improving customer retention.

2. Aligning Data Projects with Strategic Objectives: To overcome the challenge of misaligned priorities, data teams should work closely with business leaders to ensure that their projects are aligned with the company's strategic objectives. This can be achieved through the use of frameworks such as Objectives and Key Results (OKRs), which help align data initiatives with specific business goals. For example, if the company's primary objective is to increase customer lifetime value (CLTV), the data team's projects should focus on identifying high-value customers, predicting churn, and recommending strategies for increasing retention. By aligning data projects with business goals, data scientists can ensure that their work has a direct impact on the company's success.

3. Breaking Down Silos with Data Integration: To overcome the issue of fragmented data, organizations should invest in data integration technologies that centralize data from different departments into a single, unified platform. This might involve adopting cloud-based data platforms, data lakes, or enterprise data warehouses that allow data scientists to access and analyze data from across the organization. For instance, a company might integrate its CRM, ERP, and marketing analytics systems into a unified data warehouse, allowing data scientists to analyze customer data, sales performance, and marketing campaign results in one place. This integration enables more comprehensive analyses that align with the company's strategic goals.

4. Fostering a Data-Driven Culture: Overcoming resistance to data-driven decision-making requires a cultural shift within the organization. Business leaders must actively promote the use of data in decision-making and demonstrate the value of data-driven insights through their own actions. This cultural shift can be facilitated through data literacy training, where employees at all levels of the organization learn how to interpret data, ask the right questions, and apply data-driven insights to their work. Additionally, creating success stories by showcasing how data initiatives have improved business outcomes can help build trust in data and reduce resistance to change. For example, a company might highlight a successful data-driven project that led to a significant increase in sales or a reduction in operational costs. By showcasing these wins, business leaders can demonstrate the value of data science and encourage more widespread adoption of data-driven practices.

5. Ensuring Data Quality: To ensure that data projects are based on reliable insights, organizations must prioritize data quality. This involves implementing data governance policies, data cleansing processes, and continuous monitoring to ensure that data is accurate, complete, and up to date. Data quality is particularly important for predictive models and advanced analytics. If the data used for training machine learning models is flawed, the insights generated will be unreliable. Organizations should invest in data quality tools and processes to ensure that their data science efforts are based on accurate information. For instance, a financial institution might implement a data quality program that includes regular audits of customer data, automated data cleansing processes, and ongoing monitoring to identify and resolve data quality issues. By ensuring data quality, the institution can make more informed decisions based on accurate insights.

6. Improving Communication Between Data Teams and Business Leaders: To bridge the communication gap between data scientists and business leaders, data teams must focus on translating technical results into business outcomes. This involves framing data insights in terms of their impact on key business metrics, such as revenue growth, cost reduction, or customer satisfaction. Data scientists should avoid overwhelming business leaders with technical jargon or overly complex models. Instead, they should focus on delivering clear, actionable insights that directly address the company's strategic goals. Using data visualization tools, such as dashboards and reports, can also help communicate complex insights in a more accessible way. For example, instead of presenting detailed model performance metrics, a data scientist might summarize the results by saying, "Our model predicts that by targeting high-value customers with personalized offers, we can increase customer retention by 15%, potentially adding $2 million in annual revenue." This clear, results-oriented communication helps business leaders understand the value of the data project and make informed decisions.

Overcoming Alignment Challenges at Airbnb

Airbnb provides a powerful example of how an organization can overcome the challenges of aligning data science with business goals. In the early years of the company, Airbnb faced significant challenges in using data effectively to drive business growth. The company's data was scattered across multiple systems, and there was a disconnect between the data team and business leaders. To address these challenges, Airbnb invested in creating a centralized data platform that integrated data from across the organization, including booking data, customer interactions, and marketing campaigns. This platform allowed data scientists to access a unified view of the business and develop more comprehensive insights. Airbnb also worked to bridge the gap between data teams and business leaders by implementing a data-driven culture. The company provided data literacy training to employees at all levels, ensuring that everyone understood how to use data in decision-making. Business leaders actively promoted data-driven initiatives, setting the expectation that all decisions would be backed by data. One of Airbnb's most successful data-driven projects involved optimizing its search ranking algorithm.

By analyzing user behavior and booking data, the data team developed an algorithm that improved the relevance of search results, leading to a significant increase in bookings and customer satisfaction. This project was successful because it was directly aligned with the company's strategic goal of improving the user experience and driving growth. Aligning data science with business goals is a complex but critical process for ensuring that data initiatives deliver real value to the organization. By addressing challenges such as misaligned priorities, organizational silos, resistance to change, and data quality issues, data scientists and business leaders can work together to create data-driven strategies that drive growth, improve efficiency, and enhance competitive advantage. As we move into the final chapter of this book, we will explore the future of data science in business strategy, examining emerging trends, technologies, and the evolving role of data scientists as strategic leaders within their organizations. But the foundation of all successful data initiatives is alignment—ensuring that data efforts are closely tied to the company's strategic objectives and lead to meaningful business outcomes.

CHAPTER 10

The Future of Data Science in Strategic Roles

A s data science continues to evolve and embed itself more deeply in business operations, its role in shaping the future of organizational strategy will only grow. Companies that harness the power of data to make informed, forward-looking decisions are better positioned to stay competitive, anticipate market shifts, and innovate at a faster pace. In this final chapter, we will explore the future of data science in strategic roles, looking at emerging trends, new technologies, and the evolving expectations for data scientists as leaders within their organizations. We will also examine how businesses can prepare for the future by building agile, data-driven cultures, investing in the next generation of tools and methodologies, and nurturing a new breed of data scientists who not only excel at technical analysis but also thrive as strategic thinkers and business partners.

Emerging Trends in Data Science

The landscape of data science is rapidly changing, driven by technological advancements and evolving business needs. Several key trends are reshaping how data scientists contribute to strategic decision-making and how organizations can leverage data to drive long-term success.

1. Real-Time Analytics and Decision-Making: As businesses increasingly operate in dynamic environments, the demand for real-time data analytics is growing. Instead of relying on historical data and periodic reports, companies now seek to make decisions based on live data, allowing them to react quickly to changing market conditions, customer behaviors, and operational challenges. Real-time analytics has broad applications across industries. In retail, for example, companies can use real-time data to optimize pricing based on customer demand and competitor actions. In finance, real-time fraud detection models help prevent fraudulent transactions before they occur. In manufacturing, real-time monitoring of production processes enables proactive maintenance, reducing downtime and increasing efficiency. For data scientists, the shift toward real-time analytics means developing models and systems that can process and analyze large volumes of data on the fly. It also requires a shift in mindset—from generating reports after the fact to influencing decisions as they happen.

2. AI-Driven Automation of Data Science: Advances in artificial intelligence (AI) and machine learning are enabling greater automation of data science workflows. AI-driven tools are increasingly capable of automating tasks such as data cleaning, feature engineering, and even model selection, reducing the time and effort required to develop data-driven solutions. This trend, often referred to as "auto-ML" (automated machine learning), allows data scientists to focus on more strategic activities, such as interpreting results, developing actionable insights, and collaborating with business leaders. By automating routine tasks, companies can also democratize data science, enabling non-technical employees to use AI-powered tools to analyze data and generate insights without needing to write complex code. For example, Google's AutoML platform allows users with limited coding experience to build custom machine learning models. As these tools become more sophisticated, data scientists will increasingly act as overseers of AI-driven systems, ensuring that the models align with business goals and are free from bias or ethical concerns.

3. The Integration of AI and Machine Learning in Business Processes: AI and machine learning are becoming integral to a wide range of business processes, from customer service automation and personalized marketing to predictive maintenance and financial forecasting. The use of AI is shifting from experimental pilot projects to core business functions, and data scientists are expected to lead this transition by developing, deploying, and optimizing AI-driven solutions. For instance, many customer service departments now use AI-powered chatbots to handle routine inquiries, freeing up human agents to focus on more complex issues. In marketing, AI models analyze customer data to deliver highly personalized offers and recommendations. In operations, predictive analytics help companies forecast demand, optimize inventory, and improve supply chain resilience. Data scientists will need to collaborate closely with IT, operations, and business teams to ensure that AI systems are integrated seamlessly into existing processes and aligned with strategic priorities. This shift will require not only technical expertise but also strong leadership and project management skills.

The Evolving Role of Data Scientists as Strategic Leaders

As data science becomes more integral to business strategy, the role of data scientists is evolving beyond technical analysis. Data scientists are increasingly expected to take on leadership roles, influencing decision-making at the highest levels of the organization. This shift is transforming data scientists into strategic leaders who can bridge the gap between data-driven insights and business execution.

1. **Data Scientists as Business Partners**: In the past, data scientists were often seen as specialists brought in to solve specific technical problems. Today, however, data scientists are becoming trusted business partners who work alongside executives to shape strategy,

drive innovation, and ensure that data is integrated into every aspect of the business. This shift requires data scientists to develop a strong understanding of business fundamentals, including financial metrics, customer behavior, market dynamics, and competitive pressures. It also requires the ability to translate complex data insights into clear, actionable recommendations that align with the company's strategic goals. For example, a data scientist working for a retail company might collaborate with the CEO, CFO, and marketing team to develop a data-driven strategy for expanding into new markets. By analyzing customer demographics, purchasing behaviors, and competitive landscapes, the data scientist can provide insights that guide decisions about product offerings, pricing strategies, and marketing campaigns.

2. Cross-Functional Leadership: As data becomes a core asset for organizations, data scientists are increasingly expected to take on cross-functional leadership roles. This involves leading data initiatives that span multiple departments, such as marketing, sales, product development, and operations, and ensuring that data insights are integrated into decision-making processes across the organization. For instance, a data scientist leading a customer retention initiative might need to collaborate with the marketing team to develop personalized retention campaigns, work with the customer service team to improve support for high-risk customers, and partner with the finance team to measure the financial impact of these efforts. In this role, the data scientist acts as a coordinator, bringing together different departments to execute a cohesive, data-driven strategy.

3. Communication and Influence: The ability to communicate complex data insights to non-technical stakeholders is becoming an increasingly important skill for data scientists. As data scientists take on more strategic roles, they must be able to present their findings in a way that resonates with business leaders, board members, and investors. This involves not only simplifying technical concepts but also framing insights in terms of business impact—how data-driven decisions can increase revenue, reduce costs, improve customer satisfaction, or enhance operational efficiency. Data scientists must also be skilled at influencing decision-makers, ensuring that data insights are translated into action. For example, when presenting a predictive model that forecasts customer churn, the data scientist might explain how the model can help the company reduce churn by 10%, saving millions in lost revenue. By connecting data insights to tangible business outcomes, data scientists can build trust and influence within the organization.

4. Continuous Learning and Adaptability: The pace of change in data science is rapid, with new tools, techniques, and technologies emerging regularly. To stay relevant and effective, data scientists must commit to continuous learning and professional development. This includes staying up to date with the latest advancements in machine learning, AI, and data engineering, as well as developing new skills in areas such as leadership, project management, and strategic thinking. In addition to technical skills, data scientists must be adaptable, ready to pivot as business needs change. Whether it's adjusting a predictive model based on new market conditions or incorporating feedback from business leaders into a data-driven strategy, adaptability will be key to success in a fast-moving, data-driven world.

Preparing for the Future: Building Agile, Data-Driven Organizations

As data science becomes a strategic asset for businesses, organizations must prepare for the future by fostering agile, data-driven cultures that empower employees at all levels to use data in decision-making. Below are some key steps businesses can take to prepare for the future of data science.

1. Investing in Data Infrastructure and Tools: To fully leverage the potential of data science, companies must invest in modern data infrastructure and tools that enable real-time data analysis, AI-driven automation, and seamless data integration across departments. This includes adopting cloud-based data platforms, machine learning platforms, and data visualization tools that democratize access to data and insights. For example, companies like Amazon and Netflix have invested heavily in cloud-based data platforms that enable real-time data processing and analysis, allowing them to respond quickly to customer behaviors and market changes.

2. Building a Data-Driven Culture: Creating a data-driven culture requires more than just hiring data scientists—it involves embedding data into the fabric of the organization. This means fostering a culture where data is valued, understood, and used by employees at all levels. To build a data-driven culture, companies should invest in data literacy training, encourage cross-functional collaboration, and promote transparency in data-driven decision-making. By empowering employees to use data in their daily work, organizations can create a culture of innovation, agility, and continuous improvement. For example, Google has built a data-driven culture where employees are encouraged to experiment with data, test new ideas, and use data to make decisions. This culture of data-driven innovation has helped Google stay at the forefront of the tech industry.

3. Nurturing the Next Generation of Data Scientists: As the demand for data scientists continues to grow, companies must invest in developing the next generation of data professionals. This includes providing opportunities for continuous learning, mentorship, and career development. In addition to technical training, companies should focus on developing the leadership and strategic skills of their data scientists. This involves providing opportunities for data scientists to take on cross-functional leadership roles, work closely with business leaders, and participate in strategic decision-making. By nurturing data scientists who excel at both technical analysis and business strategy, companies can build a workforce that is prepared to lead in a data-driven future.

The Future of Data Science in Business Strategy

The future of data science is bright, and its role in shaping business strategy will only continue to expand. As AI, machine learning, and real-time analytics become more advanced, data scientists will play an increasingly important role in driving innovation, optimizing operations, and guiding strategic decision-making. To succeed in this evolving landscape, data scientists must not only master technical skills but also develop a deep understanding of business strategy, cross-functional collaboration, and leadership. They must become trusted partners to business leaders, helping to navigate the complexities of a data-driven world and turn insights into action. As we look to the future, businesses that embrace data science as a core component of their strategy will be better positioned to thrive in a fast-paced, competitive environment. By building agile, data-driven organizations, investing in cutting-edge tools, and nurturing the next generation of data scientists, companies can unlock the full potential of data science and lead the way into the future of business.